In Pursuit of Truth:

Separating Fact from Folklore in Forensic Science

Susan petricia. J

Published by **SPI Publications**, www.spipublications.in

SPI, the **SPI logo**, and **Split Poetry India** are trademarks of **SPI Publications**, or its affiliates.

ISBN-13: 978-93-49860-47-6

First Edition 2025

SPI Publications

Corporate & Editorial Office

117/2, Sector 37, Khandsa Road,
Gurgaon, Haryana 122 001
Phone: +91 98355 52940
Email: contact@spipublications.in
Website: www.spipublications.in

Processed and Printed in India

Dedication

To the seekers of truth,

To the silent evidence that always speaks,

And to every student who dares to look closer

This book is for you.

Epigraph

~Not every healer operates on bodies—some heal through fairness.

Foreword

It is both a privilege and a moment of quiet pride to introduce this exceptional work, In Pursuit of Truth, authored by my student, Ms. Susan Petricia J., a second-year undergraduate in Forensic Science. This book is more than a compilation of concepts and case studies—it is a statement. A statement from a young mind willing to challenge myths, clarify science, and courageously step into the complex terrain where justice meets evidence.

In a world captivated by television thrillers and fictional portrayals of forensic magic, Susan's work offers something much rarer: clarity, honesty, and scientific integrity. Page by page, she peels back the dramatized layers and introduces readers to the real world of forensic science—where truth is earned through discipline, not drama.

What is remarkable is not just her grasp of advanced forensic themes—DNA fallacies, instrument limitations, pathology misconceptions—but her determination to write a book at this stage of her academic journey. That speaks of maturity and mission. It reflects a commitment to knowledge that goes far beyond classroom boundaries.

As a teacher, I have watched Susan evolve from a curious student to a thoughtful analyst. Her diligence, sincerity, and resilience are evident not only in her questions during lectures but also in the rigor with which she has approached this publication. The structure of the chapters, the inclusion of expert voices, the real-world case studies—all point to a future forensic professional in the making.

This book will serve as a compass for aspiring students, educators, and even practitioners who seek to revisit foundational truths in forensic science. More importantly, it is a reminder that scientific thinking must always triumph over assumptions, and that even the youngest voices in academia have something vital to say.

I commend Susan for this effort and hope that this work inspires many more students to question, explore, and above all—pursue truth.

Dr. Aslam Moideen C A

Head, Department of Criminology and Forensic Science

Nehru Arts and Science College

Acknowledgement

First and foremost, I express my sincere thanks to the Almighty God for His blessings, support, and strength during this journey. This work would not have been achievable without His grace.

I extend my heartfelt thanks to my family for their constant support, understanding, and encouragement throughout the many hours of research and writing.

I want to extend my heartfelt gratitude to my Head of Department and all my mentors whose wisdom and support motivated me to pursue this project with enthusiasm and commitment.

In closing, I express my gratitude to each reader who engages with this book, wishing it provides insight and motivates your search for truth in the intriguing realm of forensic science.

Special thanks to all the forensic experts for contributing in the expert Q&A.

Mr. Nidhin SS

Ms. Dinsha K

Ms. Dhanya R

Ms. Reshma santhosh

Mr. Harsha vardhan Dasari

Mr. Saurav kumar

Dr. Richa Rohatgi

Piyush Kumar

Darshan rs

Venkat Gangadari

Aryasree A

Anurag dubey

Archana Sunil

Manju

Author's Note

This book has been written as a personal and professional endeavor, seeking to analyze the silent evidence found at crime scenes and the scientific principles that enable them to speak.

Tales whispered through blood patterns, woven through fibers, and concealed within fingerprints. I've tried to tell those stories in this book using facts, cases, and the fundamental methods that make forensic investigation such a potent instrument for justice—rather than using fiction.

The chapters are organized to walk you through fundamental ideas, backed up by real-world case studies, myth-busting facts, and the ever-changing technologies that influence contemporary forensic practice. I hope this book gives you the clarity, curiosity, and confidence to pursue the truth with integrity, regardless of whether you are a student, an enthusiast, or an aspiring investigator.

The truth leaves a trail. I hope this one does as well.

Context

CHAPTER 1

Introduction- Fact Vs Forensic Fiction

Forensic science has gained widespread popularity because to its romanticization in literature, film, television, and most lately, the news media. It is easy to appeal to a broad audience since forensic science is just fascinating and exciting. In order to piece together the specifics of the crime, the fictitious forensic scientist gathers evidence at crime sites, examines it in a state-of-the-art laboratory, and applies objective science. It's a really fulfilling tale. Science reveals the truth and exposes falsehoods. Justice is done when the criminal are convicted and the innocent are let free.

Many of the characteristics that made forensic science so alluring in this fictitious context are still present in the actual world. In the actual world, criminal prosecutions do involve scientific examination of tangible evidence

Yet, the public and, more crucially, aspiring forensic science students are rarely exposed to real forensic work through popular media. Having a better understanding of what forensic science is and is not, as well as what its practitioners must do, is crucial when thinking about a career in the field.

The main character utilizes science as a tricks, a technical tool, to uncover evidence that the criminal undoubtedly believed would go unnoticed.

In practice, forensic scientists interact with evidence gathered from places of crime in the lab for extended periods of time. The objective of the forensic scientist is to evaluate the evidence that has been given objectively and provide the investigator with an interpretation. The majority of forensic scientists process evidence in labs, while there are chances for investigative field-based work.

Although the work is as hard as it would be in any other analytical lab, the scientist is rarely required to outsmart or track down criminals.

Even with these widespread misunderstandings, working in forensics may still be rather fulfilling. Unlike other scientists, forensic scientists can often follow both the laboratory analysis of evidence and the courtroom interpretation of the analytical results in their cases.analytical laboratories that can be assembling a tiny component of a bigger puzzle.

Incorrect assumptions concerning forensic education stem from a misunderstanding of the work of forensic scientists. Students who are tired of the"hard"sciences might believe that they can work in forensics without having to undergo the rigorous training needed for more conventional science fields. This isn't true. It is important for potential pupils to understand that forensic scientists are scientists first and foremost.

Chemists and biologists who have received further training in applying their scientific knowledge to forensics and the criminal justice system are known as forensic scientists. In fact, it would be unacceptable if the forensic scientists who assist in resolving problems in the criminal justice system lacked the scientific expertise of those employed in comparable analytical labs.

In addition to possessing extensive fundamental knowledge and expertise, the forensic scientist must be aware of the current practices in the area and comprehend the scientific concepts that underlie them. The forensic scientist will only be able to choose the most effective technique for examining different kinds of evidence after they have a firm grasp of both the fundamental science and the nature of forensic science.

Serious scientists who want to use their expertise in an area that directly advances justice and benefits society should pursue forensic science.

CHAPTER 2

The Fallacy of Immediate Justice: Laboratory Work Isn't Like Television

Many times, forensic science is presented as a quick process in which a single expert can solve complete cases and findings are visible in a matter of minutes. Laboratory-based forensic investigations are actually difficult, exhausting, and entail a number of specialists and processes. This chapter explains the complex reality of forensic analysis and explains why it takes a long time.

1. ***The fallacy in Media*** :

TV shows frequently show forensic experts getting samples, running them through a machine, and quickly obtaining a conclusive match. To guarantee the validity of the results, forensic labs really adhere to a chain of custody, defined procedures, and quality assurance inspections. For narrative purposes, the dramatization omits or simplifies necessary steps.

2. ***Intake and Registration of Evidence*** :

Evidence is not examined right away after it arrives at the forensic lab. It first goes through classification, paperwork, and registration. To guarantee that the evidence is kept untouched, a chain of custody is put in place. In busy labs that handle dozens of cases every day, this documentation alone can take several hours.

3. ***Setting priorities and caseload*** : Forensic labs frequently handle an excessive number of cases. Samples are prioritized according to court requests, legal deadlines, or case urgency rather than being analyzed in the order they come. Time-sensitive cases are given priority over cold cases, which may be shifted down the list. This leads to a backlog at many public forensic labs.

4. ***The Methodical Analysis Procedure*** :

Every forensic test has multiple steps,

Screening:

The existence of pertinent substances (such as blood, drugs, or toxins) is determined by preliminary tests.

Extraction and preparation process:

Chemical or biological materials are separated, cleaned, and ready for examination as part of the extraction and preparation process. To prevent erroneous results, contaminants are eliminated.

Instrumental Analysis:

High-tech tools such as FTIR, GC-MS, and LC-MS are employed. These tests need calibration and quality control, and they take a lot of time.

Interpretation of the Data:

The findings are not always definitive. Chromatograms, spectra, and DNA electropherograms must be interpreted by analysts, who frequently compare the results to reference standards.

5. ***Reporting and Documentation*** :

After analysis, forensic scientists are required to write comprehensive reports that include their methodology, results, limits, and conclusions. These documents are legal records that can be produced in court; they are not just summaries. Additional testing might be necessary if discrepancies are discovered or defense attorneys ask for more details.

6. ***Peer supervision and review :***

Peer review is required in many labs before results are finalized. To ensure neutrality and correctness, the interpretation is verified by a second qualified analyst or supervisor. This additional layer aids in preventing erroneous convictions in delicate instances.

7. ***Difficulties and Hold-Ups*** :

Frequently, forensic labs lack sufficient funding and personnel. Analysts balance a variety of duties, including casework, administrative work, trial testimony, and training. Further delays may be caused by sample contamination, equipment failures, or ambiguous results.

8. ***A Group-Based Initiative :***

Real cases require cooperation, in contrast to the fiction of a single expert handling everything: Officers at crime scenes gather and package evidence. Various departments examine evidence that is digital, physical, chemical, or biological. The story is constructed by law enforcement officials using a variety of sources. This collaboration demonstrates the complexity and interdependence of forensic investigation.

9. ***Actual Case Study***:

The Gang Rape Case in Delhi (2012) Although forensic testing was essential in the Nirbhaya case, the outcomes were not immediate. Despite the national concern, it took weeks to complete the toxicological and DNA reports. To ensure that results would stand up in court, the lab had to follow a rigorous methodology. This delay resulted from following legal and scientific requirements rather than from inefficiency.

10. ***Precision Rather Than Velocity*** :

Both the public and the legal system have irrational expectations as a result of the illusion of fast justice. It may result in forensic scientists being under excessive pressure and in court proceedings being uninformed. In actuality, forensic science values accuracy, verification, and ethical responsibility much like any other science. When justice is handled properly, it becomes a potent ally of the truth; when it is hurried, it runs the risk of being compromised.

CHAPTER 3

Not Every DNA Sample Is a Smoking Gun.

DNA is a highly effective instrument in forensic science, yet it is also one of the most misinterpreted. DNA evidence is frequently presented in the media as infallible and unquestionable, which causes a number of misunderstandings.

This chapter dispels common misconceptions about DNA analysis and outlines the intricate workings of the field.

1. ***Myth*** : ***A complete, unambiguous profile is always provided by DNA.***

Reality : Many people think that any biological evidence recovered from a crime scene always yields a complete genetic profile for forensic specialists. It's hardly the case in action, though. Heat, humidity, and time are some of the environmental conditions that cause many DNA samples to degrade. Additionally, there might not be enough DNA to create a complete profile, or the DNA might be combined with that of other people. The strength of the inferences that can be derived is diminished and interpretation becomes more complicated when only partial profiles are acquired.

2. ***Myth*** : ***A defendant is convicted if their DNA matches***

Reality : When a suspect's DNA matches a sample recovered from a crime scene, it suggests that the suspect may have given the DNA.It does not, however, provide information on how, when, or why the DNA was deposited. DNA is a persistent molecule and can remain on surfaces for long periods of time. It can also be transferred indirectly through shared objects, environments, or other individuals. Therefore, presence of DNA at a scene does not prove involvement in a crime without supporting context from other evidence.

3. ***Myth : It only takes one DNA test.***

Reality : DNA testing is a multi-step and multi-shot procedure. Particularly in complicated situations involving DNA combinations from numerous individuals, it necessitates meticulous validation and frequently several testing cycles. To guarantee consistency, the first test results are frequently confirmed by additional testing. Additionally, analysts verify the veracity of all findings by comparing them to established standards and controls and having senior analysts or supervisors examine them. Although it requires time and resources, this multi-layered procedure guarantees dependability.

4. ***Myth : Touch DNA is consistently trustworthy.***

Reality: Skin cells that are left over after a brief encounter with an object are collected for touch DNA analysis. Despite its high sensitivity, this approach is susceptible to contamination and misunderstanding. For instance, when someone touches anything, their DNA may be unintentionally passed to another person. If this secondary transfer is not thoroughly examined, it may lead to false findings. Furthermore, the amount of DNA retrieved could be so small that it produces incomplete or unclear profiles that are impossible to analyze with certainty.

5. ***Myth*** : ***DNA has an eternal lifespan.***

Reality : DNA does not stay intact indefinitely, despite what many people believe. Over time, it deteriorates, particularly when exposed to environmental elements including moisture, light, and heat. Improper storage of biological samples can cause them to degrade, making it difficult or impossible to extract useful DNA. Even when DNA can be recovered, data from degraded samples is frequently insufficient or of poor quality. As a result, in forensic investigations, prompt and appropriate sample preservation is essential.

6. ***Myth*** : ***DNA testing is rapid.***

Reality : The process of analyzing DNA is lengthy and involves several stages: extraction of the DNA from the sample, quantification to measure how much DNA is present, amplification of the DNA using polymerase chain reaction (PCR), separation and detection using capillary electrophoresis, and finally, interpretation of the data. Each step must be performed meticulously and is often repeated if quality control fails. Moreover, labs may have significant backlogs, meaning it can take weeks or even months to obtain final results.

7. ***Myth : DNA can't be incorrect.***

Reality : Although DNA is a strong tool, it is not perfect. Any step of the analysis process is susceptible to errors. These include tainted samples, incorrect collection, incorrect labeling, broken equipment, or human mistake in interpretation. The risk is in assuming that DNA evidence is infallible. To guarantee that the results are as accurate and trustworthy as possible, stringent procedures, peer evaluations, and accreditation criteria are in place. Nevertheless, mistakes have been made in actual cases despite all the precautions, occasionally leading to erroneous convictions.

An Actual Case Study: Heilbronn's Phantom

One of the most peculiar and illuminating forensic blunders in the history of contemporary criminal investigations is the"Phantom of Heilbronn"case. More than 40 crime locations in Germany, Austria, and France were involved in this 15-year-long investigation, which started in 1993 and was purportedly connected by a single, enigmatic female DNA profile.

The Enigma Emerges

The case started when detectives found the same female DNA profile at several crime locations, including drug-related offenses, murders, and burglaries. These crimes had rather distinct victims and situations, and they took place in quite separate places. Most famously, the DNA was discovered at the scene of a German police officer's 2007 murder in Heilbronn, which brought the case to the attention of the country.

The enigmatic woman who provided the DNA was dubbed"The Woman Without a Face"or"The Phantom of Heilbronn"as the investigation went on. Her DNA was found in a startling range of places, including a burned-out caravan, a bullet case, and a toy gun used in a crime. Both law enforcement and forensic professionals were perplexed by her ability to appear everywhere while remaining unseen to cameras and witnesses.

Theories and Investigative Confusion

Investigators believed they were tracking down a female serial killer. They speculated that she might be a member of an organized crime syndicate, a master of disguise, or a vagrant. Numerous crime scenes were linked by this one DNA profile, which prompted extensive manhunts, international collaboration, psychological profiling, and even the participation of leading criminal profilers. The mystery was increased by the fact that the profile did not correspond to any recognized people in criminal databases. The notion of this elusive, unseen woman committing crimes across Europe captivated the public and media.

The Turn: A Forensic Discovery

Then everything fell apart in 2009. The startling conclusion of a thorough internal inquiry was that the DNA did not actually belong to a criminal. It was instead linked to a female employee of the facility that produced the cotton swabs used to gather DNA evidence. Despite being utilized for forensic crime scene samples, these cotton swabs were not sterile. During packaging, her DNA had tainted the swabs. Even though the employee had never been involved in any criminal activity, her DNA was found at every crime site since the same set of swabs had been sent to police agencies across the globe.

The Heilbronn Phantom case turned into a potent illustration of how forensic evidence may mislead an entire inquiry if it is gathered or interpreted incorrectly. It revealed serious problems with quality control, erroneous assumptions in DNA interpretation, and an over dependence on DNA as unquestionable evidence. Consequently, the case resulted in significant forensic scientific procedural revisions throughout Europe. Authorities stressed strict contamination avoidance procedures and required the use of certified sterile, DNA-free consumables.

A lesson in forensic science can be learned from the Phantom of Heilbronn case. It shows how oversight and human mistake, even something as basic as using non-sterile equipment, may produce intricate illusions and lead investigators astray for years. It also serves as a reminder that the quality of science depends on how it is applied. DNA evidence is powerful, but it must be examined carefully, according to quality standards, and with scientific skepticism.

In conclusion, The Phantom of Heilbronn case is a cautionary tale in forensic science. It illustrates how human error and oversight — even something as simple as using non-sterile equipment — can create elaborate illusions and send investigators down the wrong path for years. It also reminds us that science is only as reliable as the methods used to apply it. Despite the power of DNA evidence, it must be interpreted within context, with strict adherence to quality standards and scientific skepticism.

The Context Is Crucial

A fundamental component of forensic science, DNA analysis needs to be applied carefully and contextually. Serious injustices can result from misinterpreting the results or from having too much faith in them. It is possible to properly utilize DNA evidence in the legal system and make sure that it advances the cause of truth rather than confusion by being aware of its advantages and disadvantages.

CHAPTER 4

What Instruments Actually Do in Crime-Spectrometers, and Chromatographs.

The reality is much more complex, even though forensic tools like spectrometers and chromatographs are frequently romanticized as miraculous devices that solve crimes. Despite their great power, these instruments need to be handled carefully, calibrated, and interpreted correctly. The main misconceptions about forensic tools used in chemical and toxicological investigation are dispelled in this chapter.

1. ***Myth*** : ***When a button is pressed, instruments automatically identify chemicals.***

Reality : Forensic analysts in crime shows can quickly identify a mystery chemical by pressing a button. In actuality, devices like Infrared Spectrometers (IR), Mass Spectrometers (MS), and Gas Chromatographs (GC) cannot "name" a substance for you. They generate unprocessed data that needs to be interpreted, like graphs, peaks, and spectra. A GC-MS, for instance, separates the compounds in a sample and produces a mass spectrum that needs to be compared to established standards. The identity of the substance is decided by the analyst, not the computer.

2. ***Myth : A single test is sufficient to verify a substance's existence.***

Reality: A material cannot be definitively confirmed by a single device in every situation. Presumptive tests, including color tests, and confirmatory tests, such GC-MS, HPLC, and FTIR, are frequently used in combination by forensic scientists. Only a confirmatory test can unequivocally determine its identity, even though a presumptive test may provide a preliminary indication—for example, that cocaine may be present. By using a tiered approach, false positives are prevented and accuracy is guaranteed.

3. ***Myth : Chromatography and spectroscopy consistently produce unambiguous results.***

Reality: When samples are deteriorated, polluted, or mixed, the actual data from these devices may be noisy, unclear, or inconclusive. For example, overlapping peaks can happen in gas chromatography when there are several compounds present with comparable retention durations. Determining if a peak represents a particular molecule and whether more purification or analysis is required requires a skilled analyst.

4. ***Myth : Instrument results can't be wrong.***

Reality : Errors can happen even with sophisticated instruments because of poor sample handling, instrument failure, inaccurate calibration, or analyst mistake. For instance, contamination may result from carry-over, or residues from earlier samples. To make sure the instrument is operating correctly and the results are trustworthy, analysts must regularly run controls, blanks, and standards. Quality control and chain-of-custody are essential for confirming findings.

5. ***Myth : Chromatography and spectroscopy operate instantaneously.***

Reality: Sample preparation can take hours, whereas data collection in devices like HPLC or GC may only take minutes. Extraction, dilution, filtration, and occasionally derivatization (chemical modification for improved detection) are the steps. Following analysis, scientists have to produce reports, interpret the findings, and frequently conduct additional experiments for confirmation. Depending on the intricacy and volume, the complete procedure may take hours or days.

6. ***Myth : It is simple to test and identify any unknown sample.***

Reality : The testing process becomes much more complicated if the analyst is unsure of what they are searching for. Different extraction methods and equipment configurations are needed for different compounds. To isolate and identify every component, unknown combinations might need to go through several rounds of analysis using several platforms (e.g., GC-MS, LC-MS/MS, FTIR). When there is no benchmark to measure against, the procedure can be time-consuming.

7. ***Myth :Human bias is eliminated by machines.***

Reality: Humans set up, analyze, and derive results from instruments; they are merely tools. In a badly maintained lab or in the hands of an untrained analyst, the same sample may produce various results. Peer evaluations, blind competency exams, and established processes are therefore required to minimize prejudice and preserve credibility.

An Actual Case Study: A Wrongful Conviction Due to Drug Analysis.

A man was mistakenly convicted in a Texas case in 2014 because a presumptive field drug test misidentified a powdered substance as methamphetamine. Prior to the trial, no chromatographic or spectroscopic confirmatory test was conducted. A GC-MS examination conducted years later confirmed that the material was, in fact, powdered aspirin. This example demonstrates why advanced tools—and more importantly, how to utilize them properly—are essential in forensic toxicology and emphasizes the risk of depending too much on preliminary testing.

The Presumptive Test and Arrest

During a routine traffic stop in 2014, Texas police stopped George Rodriguez. Officers discovered a little plastic bag containing a white powdered substance when searching the vehicle. They used a presumptive field test, which is based on a chemical reagent that changes color when specific substances are present, as is customary. When the methamphetamine test came back positive, Rodriguez was immediately taken into custody for narcotics possession. At the time of his trial, there was no laboratory analysis to support the field test kit, despite its speed and convenience.

The Verdict Without Confirmatory Evidence

The court acknowledged the field test result as adequate proof, even though Rodriguez said the powder was just crushed aspirin he used to treat headaches. During his trial, no confirmatory laboratory test, such as Gas Chromatography-Mass Spectrometry (GC-MS), was performed or provided. This mistake turned out to be crucial. Because it can accurately identify chemical structures and rule out false positives, GC-MS is regarded as the gold standard in forensic drug analysis. Because of its absence, Rodriguez was found guilty only on the basis of a general, presumptive test. He received a prison sentence, adding his name to a lengthy list of those who have been imprisoned as a result of poor forensic procedures.

GC-MS's Function in Revealing the Truth

Rodriguez's case was examined by the Texas Forensic Science Commission years later as part of a larger inquiry into erroneous convictions stemming from field tests. The panel mandated a GC-MS reanalysis of the material. The outcome? It was determined that the material was crushed aspirin, an entirely safe and legal over-the-counter drug. No illegal drugs, including methamphetamine, were detected. The fact that Rodriguez had been unfairly convicted and had done time for a non-crime was reinforced by this revelation.

The Systemic Problem

Rodriguez's situation wasn't unusual. Hundreds of convictions nationwide were based solely on erroneous field drug tests, according to a 2016 New York Times investigation. Although these presumptive kits are commonly used and reasonably priced, they have a history of producing false positive results when used with simple compounds like soap, sugar, and pharmaceuticals. Unreliable evidence was used to imprison innocent persons at the time since many countries did not require confirmatory tests prior to charging someone or holding a trial.

The story of George Rodriguez is a potent warning. It illustrates how lives can be destroyed by the improper use of forensic tools or, worse, by their non-use. The truth is in the intricacies of forensic science, and it is never acceptable to omit appropriate analysis.

Crimes are solved by people, not by tools.

Although they are extremely important, forensic tools are not perfect. They need to be operated, interpreted, and contextually understood by skilled humans. Chromatographs and spectrometers produce facts, not judgments. They provide strong assistance in revealing the truth when paired with the appropriate approach and knowledge. However, they might confuse investigations and compromise justice if misinterpreted or abused.

CHAPTER 5

Truths about Trace Evidence: Blood, Prints, and Fibers

In a forensic inquiry, trace evidence—such as minuscule fibers, invisible fingerprints, or small drops of blood—can reveal a great deal. Though they are surrounded by misconceptions and myths, these minor hints can carry significant weight in courtrooms and the public's imagination. This chapter exposes the factual realities underlying the most widespread myths regarding fiber inspection, fingerprint recognition, and bloodstain analysis. In addition to improving investigative thinking, being aware of these facts helps one avoid the risks associated with placing undue trust in evidence that is frequently significantly more brittle than it seems.

1. ***Myth : Blood is always evidence of criminal activity.***

Reality: It is commonly assumed that the owner was involved in the crime when blood is found at the site. Blood can, however, be present for a variety of causes unrelated to criminal activity. Blood traces may be left by unintentional wounds, nosebleeds, menstrual blood, or even surgical treatments. Consequently, the mere discovery of blood is only one component of a bigger picture and does not prove guilt. To prevent drawing incorrect conclusions, forensic scientists must carefully evaluate blood evidence in light of the entire investigation.

2. ***Myth : The presence of blood is conclusively demonstrated by the Luminol test.***

Reality : A substance called luminol combines with the iron in hemoglobin to produce a luminous effect, which is used to identify blood traces. Despite its usefulness, luminol is a presumptive test instead of a conclusive one. Additionally, it can react with things like bleach, certain metals, and plant components, leading to false positive results. Thus, Luminol's light suggests that blood may be present, but additional laboratory testing, such as DNA analysis, is required to verify that the material is, in fact, blood.

3. ***Myth : At crime scenes, fingerprints are always evident.***

Reality: Not everyone leaves viable fingerprints at a crime scene, despite the fact that scientists agree that no two people have the same fingerprints. A fingerprint's ability to be deposited clearly enough for analysis depends on a number of parameters, such as the surface's texture, the amount of pressure used, the skin's state (oily or dry), and environmental factors like moisture or dust. Therefore, it is typical for fingerprints to be absent or to have imprecise prints, and investigators should not rely solely on fingerprint evidence.

4. ***Myth : Automated Fingerprint Identification Systems (AFIS) automatically generate precise matches.***

Reality *:* By scanning fingerprint databases and producing a prioritized list of potential matches, the digital technology AFIS assists forensic examiners. However, a skilled fingerprint analyst must physically review and confirm the prints in order to make a final decision of a match. AFIS is a tool that expedites the process but mainly relies on human judgment to prevent false positives; it cannot"declare"a match on its own.

5. ***Myth: A fiber match identifies a suspect in a crime with certainty.***

Reality *:* Although fibers discovered at a crime scene or on a suspect may point to a connection, they are regarded as class evidence rather than distinctive like DNA or fingerprints. Numerous fibers, like cotton and polyester, are widely available and quickly spread through shared surroundings or casual touch. Additionally, fibers have the ability to transmit secondarily, which means that even if person A had no direct contact with the murder scene, a fiber could have transferred from person B. Therefore, fiber evidence should always be interpreted cautiously and in combination with other findings.

6. ***Myth : Patterns of bloodstains make it evident how a crime was committed.***

Reality *:* Although bloodstain pattern analysis (BPA) is a potent technique for event reconstruction, it is extremely difficult and necessitates a great deal of knowledge and expertise. The patterns can be changed by a variety of parameters, including the angle of impact, blood volume, surface roughness, and ambient conditions. As a result, various specialists may have diverse interpretations of the same bloodstain pattern. Although BPA offers useful hints, conclusions should never be drawn from it alone; rather, it should be utilized in conjunction with other information.

7. ***Myth : The fingerprints of identical twins are identical.***

Reality : Identical twins have the same DNA, but each person's fingerprints are different. The reason for this uniqueness is that, in addition to heredity, random environmental factors like pressure and amniotic fluid flow during pregnancy also contribute to the formation of fingerprints. This indicates that even for identical twins, fingerprints continue to be one of the most trustworthy methods of identifying a person.

An actual case study: The Brandon Mayfield Fingerprint Controversy.

Based on fingerprint evidence, the FBI incorrectly named lawyer Brandon Mayfield as a suspect in the 2004 Madrid train bombings. A partial fingerprint found at the crime scene was compared to Mayfield's prints via AFIS. But the real suspect was later located by Spanish police. This instance demonstrated that, despite their uniqueness, fingerprints need to be carefully examined and evaluated by humans to prevent mistakes brought on by confirmation bias and partial prints. It also emphasized how crucial it is to double-check and not rely just on one piece of data.

Context: The Train Bombings in Madrid

In Madrid, Spain, commuter trains were targeted by a string of coordinated bombs on March 11, 2004, leaving 193 people dead and more than 2,000 injured. A latent fingerprint was extracted from a plastic bag discovered close to the bombing site that was purportedly filled with detonators as part of an international inquiry into the catastrophic strikes.

AFIS and Brandon Mayfield's Match

The fingerprint was run through the FBI's Automated Fingerprint Identification System (AFIS), which produced 20 possible matches. One of the results was Brandon Mayfield, a U.S. attorney and former Army officer who had converted to Islam. The FBI asserted that the fingerprint was a perfect match to Mayfield's left index finger based on the AFIS match.

Detention and Arrest

Mayfield was arrested and held for two weeks as a result of a material witness warrant. Even his office and house were secretly spied by the FBI. Only fingerprint identification made Mayfield a suspect, even though he had never been to Spain and there was no concrete evidence connecting him to the explosions.

The Reality Shows

After continuing to doubt the FBI's match, Spanish officials finally determined that the fingerprint belonged to Ouhnane Daoud, an Algerian national with documented terrorist connections who lived in Spain. The FBI was forced to admit its mistake, and Mayfield was released. After challenging the U.S. government for wrongful arrest and civil rights abuses, he received a $2 million settlement in 2006.

What Went Wrong?

Several important problems with fingerprint analysis were revealed by this case: Over-reliance on AFIS findings without enough human review Confirmation bias, since investigators might have been swayed by Mayfield's background and religion Subjectivity in comparing fingerprints, particularly when partial or smeared prints are involved It also made clear that, despite its strength, fingerprint recognition is not always accurate, particularly when taken at face value without supporting documentation.

In conclusion Although blood, fibers, and fingerprints are very useful in forensic investigations, they have limitations and need to be properly analyzed. Myths around these traces frequently originate from how they are portrayed in the media, which oversimplifies intricate scientific facts. To create a solid case, forensic specialists stress that these types of trace evidence should never be utilized alone but rather should always be supported by additional information. Knowing the facts underlying these beliefs guarantees that justice is administered using science rather than conjecture.

CHAPTER 6

Myths in Forensic Toxicology and Drug Analysis: Poisons, Pills, and Paranoia

Forensic investigations, ranging from suspicious deaths to drug-facilitated crimes and impaired driving, heavily rely on toxicology, the study of poisons, and drug analysis. Nevertheless, this area of forensics is frequently misinterpreted, with popular media and television programs spreading simplistic or inflated notions about how poisons function and how drugs are found. This chapter dispels some of the most widespread myths regarding drug analysis and forensic toxicology, substituting reality and science for fiction and terror.

1. ***Myth : Every poison kills immediately.***

Reality : The concept of an instant-death toxin is mostly made up. Depending on their dosage, mode of entrance (inhaled, swallowed, or injected), and the individual's metabolism, the majority of toxins need time to start working. Certain poisons, such as cyanide, take effect quickly, but not immediately. Others, such as arsenic or antifreeze (ethylene glycol), might be lethal or take hours or days to manifest symptoms. To ascertain how, when, and in what dosage a toxin harmed a person, forensic toxicologists rely on meticulous analysis.

2. ***Myth* : *It is usually simple to identify the presence of a drug or toxin.***

Reality : Many poisons break down quickly in the body, especially if a significant amount of time has passed between exposure and sample collection. Some substances, like certain sedatives or designer drugs, may not even be detected by routine screening unless targeted specifically. Advanced tools like GC-MS (Gas Chromatography-Mass Spectrometry) and LC-MS/MS (Liquid Chromatography) are often required, and even then, detection depends on timing, dosage, and biological factors.

3. *Myth*: ***When a toxicological test is positive, it indicates that someone was poisoned.***

Reality : Poisoning does not always occur when a substance or chemical is found in the body. Everybody's body has traces of chemicals, whether from drugs, coffee, nicotine, or simply exposure to the environment. To ascertain if a chemical caused harm or death, forensic toxicologists must take into account concentration levels, metabolite ratios, and clinical context. Forensic judgment is essential in these evaluations since, for instance, therapeutic amounts of morphine fluctuate greatly from lethal ones.

4. ***Myth* : *Results from toxicology are always 100% accurate.***

Reality : Even though toxicology is a powerful science, errors do occur. Cross-reactivity in screening tests might result in false positives. Consuming poppy seeds, for instance, may result in an opioid false positive. Strict procedures must be followed when handling samples, and testing equipment needs to be calibrated on a regular basis. Any mistake, whether technical or human, can affect the result. Forensic toxicologists therefore adhere to strict quality control protocols to guarantee that findings are both legally and scientifically sound.

5. ***Myth : Drug use in the body is evidence of guilt or intent.***

Reality : Although discovering narcotics in a victim's or suspect's body can cause serious concerns, it does not automatically mean that there was criminal intent. For example, a victim may have self-administered sleeping medications, therefore finding them in them does not prove they were poisoned by someone else. Likewise, the presence of narcotics in a suspect's system does not necessarily indicate malice. Context, witness statements, and physical evidence are necessary to demonstrate motive and causation.

6. ***Myth : Every toxicological test yields outcomes right away.***

Reality : Real toxicology analysis takes time, typically days or weeks, unlike TV crime shows. Expert interpretation and laboratory processing are necessary for cross-checking for rare compounds, confirmatory testing, and comprehensive drug panels. The timing is slower in high-stakes instances, including as overdoses or homicides, to guarantee accuracy. There are rapid tests, but they are only preliminary and provide little information.

7. ***Myths : Compared to manufactured poisons, natural poisons are less harmful.***

Reality : Some of the most lethal chemicals in forensic history are found in nature; little amounts of belladonna, aconite, curare, and ricin (castor beans) can be lethal. Natural does not equate to safety. Since many typical toxicological screenings concentrate on synthetic medicines or pharmaceuticals, these poisons are actually more difficult to find. To find and recognize plant-based poisons, experts frequently require specific training and equipment.

An actual case study: Georgi Markov's Unsolved Death- The Ricin Umbrella Assassination.

A small ricin-laced pellet fired from a modified umbrella killed Bulgarian dissident Georgi Markov in London in 1978. Shortly after experiencing a sting in his leg, he became unwell and passed away three days later. The case—which was connected to Cold War espionage—became a famous illustration of covert poisoning and brought to light the difficulties in forensic toxicology's detection of natural poisons.

The Odd Sting

Georgi Markov, a Bulgarian dissident, was strolling beside London's Waterloo Bridge in September 1978 when he felt a quick, stinging sting in his thigh. Behind him he saw a man grabbing an umbrella and hurrying off. Markov became very sick in a matter of hours, with intense agony and a high fever. After three days, he passed away under strange circumstances despite receiving medical attention.

A Tiny Pellet as a Forensic Clue

A little metal pellet was found embedded in Markov's leg during a postmortem examination. Two tiny pores in the pellet were designed to release a poisonous material gradually. Ricine, a strong plant-based poison that stops cells from producing proteins and eventually causes organ failure, was suspected by forensic scientists. But at the time, lab confirmation was quite difficult because ricin is hard to detect and breaks down quickly in the body.

A Poisonous Scheme

Investigators connected the occurrence to a clandestine killing in which the poisoned pellet was injected using a modified umbrella, a method thought to have been employed by the Bulgarian secret police with assistance from the Soviet KGB. This advanced delivery technique stunned the forensic community and brought chemical weapons usage in political executions to the attention of the world.

Teachings in Toxicology

This case, which highlights the perils of natural poisons and the inventiveness of poison delivery devices, continues to be a landmark in forensic toxicology. It underlined that not all toxins are readily traceable and that when routine tests fail to provide definitive results, a comprehensive, interdisciplinary inquiry is essential. Today, researchers continue to examine Markov's case as a cautionary tale about the potential and limitations of toxicology.

In conclusion, Clarifying drug-related crimes, exposing drunkenness, and identifying concealed causes of death all depend on forensic toxicology and drug analysis. But the science is much more complicated than what is shown in the media. Toxicology reports need to be interpreted by experts, not merely for detection, because poisons don't always act right away. Investigators and the general public might approach toxicology with reasonable expectations and scientific respect provided they are aware of its limitations, advantages, and myths.

CHAPTER 7

Echoes of the Deceased – Revealing Truths in Forensic Pathology

The reason and method of death are examined in forensic pathology.To uncover hidden realities, pathologists perform autopsies, evaluate wounds, and examine interior organs. But crime shows and thrillers have created common misunderstandings, including figuring out the time of death right away or solving every murder with a scalpel and microscope. In this chapter, the most persistent misconceptions about forensic pathology are addressed, and the actual, methodical processes of examining the dead are explained. Forensic pathologists play the role of the deceased's voice of truth when they are unable to speak.

1. ***Myth : The precise time of death can be ascertained.***

Reality : It is hard and rarely reliable to estimate the time of death. The surroundings, disease, or activity prior to death can all have an impact on factors such as body temperature (algor mortis), rigidity (rigor mortis), and lividity (livor mortis). These factors only provide approximate windows of time. Instead of providing specific hours, forensic pathologists provide estimated ranges, and even then, only with supporting data can that range become more precise.

2. ***Myth : The reason of death is always disclosed by autopsies.***

Reality : Not every death leaves obvious evidence. The body may not exhibit any outward symptoms of trauma in certain situations, such as drug overdoses, metabolic disorders, or specific cardiac diseases. Tests for toxicological and histology are crucial in these situations. Even after extensive testing, the result can occasionally be a"undetermined"cause of death, which is a valid scientific finding but frequently misinterpreted.

3. ***Myth : Bodies always seem as they do in criminal dramas.***

Reality : While TV frequently sanitizes postmortem settings, decomposition in real life is messy, unpredictable, and affected by a variety of factors, including clothes, humidity, temperature, and insects. A body left outside might quickly decay, but one kept within or in a chilly environment might stay preserved for weeks. These difficulties need forensic pathologists to overcome them with both emotional fortitude and scientific precision.

4. ***Myth : Every mark or wound shows the precise manner of death.***

Reality: Not every mark offers a complete tale, but injuries can provide important information. Similar injuries can be caused by accidents, attacks, or illnesses, and a bruise may appear before or after death. To properly diagnose trauma, pathologists must evaluate context, tissue reactions, and damage patterns. Missed discoveries or unfounded allegations may result from misinterpreting these indicators.

5. ***Myth : Only homicide cases are handled by forensic pathologists***

Reality : Forensic pathologists investigate all forms of unexpected and unexpected fatalities, including drug overdoses, accidents, suicides, unidentified illnesses, and deaths in jail, but the media concentrates on homicides. Their role is to offer objective medical causes and manners of death, which might subsequently assist law enforcement or legal proceedings, rather than to"solve murders."

6. ***Myth : Autopsy reports are quick and easy to understand***

Reality : When toxicology or specialist testing is needed, autopsy results might take weeks or even months to complete. Clinically detailed reports are frequently misinterpreted by those without medical knowledge. They are organized records that cover anatomy, organ systems, tissue samples, and expert opinions rather than merely being"crime summaries."

7. ***Myth : Detective-style testimony from forensic pathologists***

Reality : The truth is that pathologists are specialists in medicine, not law enforcement. They present unbiased, fact-based views in court that are grounded in their research rather than conjecture or indictment. They explain if injuries were compatible with self-harm, violence, accidents, or natural causes rather than deciding guilt or innocence.

An actual case study: The Mysterious Death of Kathleen Peterson – The Staircase Case

The Finding

In 2001, author Michael Peterson contacted emergency services to inform them that his wife, Kathleen Peterson, had fallen down the stairs at their home in North Carolina. Upon arrival, responders discovered her lifeless at the base of the stairs, surrounded by a significant pool of blood. The scene sparked instant doubt because of the intensity and distribution of the blood patterns.

Results of the Autopsy

The autopsy showed several cuts on the scalp, not compatible with a typical fall. There were no fractures in the skull, yet the quantity and type of injuries indicated blunt force trauma. The forensic pathologist determined the death to be a homicide, indicating that the injuries were more probably inflicted by repeated strikes rather than by falling down the stairs. Toxicology findings showed no presence of alcohol or drugs that could have led to a loss of balance.

Disputes and Challenges

The incident ignited discussion among forensic specialists. Some endorsed the murder verdict, while others contended that the blood patterns and wounds might stem from a fall, coupled with delicate blood vessels and extended bleeding. A recent theory suggested an owl assault led to Kathleen's fall. The differing interpretations highlighted how forensic pathology can provide vital—but not necessarily definitive—insights.

Influence on the Discipline

Michael Peterson was found guilty in 2003, but after many years of appeals and new evidence (which included discrediting a prosecution expert), he agreed to a plea deal in 2017. The incident, detailed in the Netflix series The Staircase, serves as a significant illustration of how the interpretations of forensic pathologists can greatly impact legal results, but remain open to scrutiny and advancing scientific understanding.

In conclusion, Forensic pathology involves asking the correct questions just as much as it involves providing answers. Distant from the exciting realm of TV dramas, actual forensic pathologists confront unpredictable timelines, decayed corpses, intricate injuries, and ambiguous findings. Their function is not to resolve crimes but to represent the deceased with scientific honesty, directing justice through evidence instead of presumption. Recognizing and honoring their constraints allows us to appreciate their input without exaggerating their influence.

CHAPTER 8

Chemical Indicators – Debunking Misconceptions in Forensic Chemistry

Forensic chemistry focuses on the identification and examination of unknown materials—whether it's a white powder found at a crime scene, traces of explosives, or paint fragments from a hit-and-run incident. It serves an essential purpose in drug analysis, toxicology, fire investigations, and examination of trace evidence. However, similar to various forensic fields, forensic chemistry is frequently misinterpreted. Media-fueled myths depict it as immediate, consistently definitive, and able to perfectly identify anything from merely "a drop of something." In truth, forensic chemistry is a very specialized area demanding systematic testing, precise analysis, and rigorous compliance with scientific procedures.

1. ***Myth : One test shows all there is to know about a substance***

Reality : There is no solitary test that can conclusively determine an unidentified material. Forensic chemists employ various methods—including chromatography, spectroscopy, mass spectrometry, and microchemical analyses—to create a comprehensive chemical profile. Results are understood as a group, not separately

2. ***Myth : Forensic chemists quickly establish the result.***

Reality : Unlike what is shown on TV, tests require time. Sample preparation, contamination management, instrument calibration, and several trial runs might be required. In actual laboratories, outcomes frequently require several days or even weeks, particularly in overwhelmed systems. Accuracy and validation take precedence over speed.

3. ***Myth : Every white powder is a drug and can be easily recognized.***

Reality : A white powder found at a location could range from sugar to fentanyl. Even chemically comparable drugs—such as heroin and morphine—necessitate thorough spectroscopic examination for distinction. Incorrect identification can lead to legal issues and health risks, making thorough verification essential.

4. ***Myth : Tracing explosive and fire residues is simple.***

Reality : Following an explosion or fire, chemical residues are frequently altered, combined, or eliminated, rendering identification highly difficult. Methods such as ion mobility spectrometry, gas chromatography-mass spectrometry (GC-MS), and residue swabbing should be employed meticulously and methodically to identify traces of accelerants or explosives.

5. ***Myth : Trace evidence like paint and soil is too insignificant to matter.***

Reality : Minute chemical remnants can connect suspects to locations or piece together occurrences. Layers of paint can correspond to a particular car model; soil tests can indicate geographic origin. Although minimal, these samples provide essential support when examined using appropriate comparative methods.

6. ***Myth : Cleaning a crime scene eliminates all chemical evidence.***

Reality : Numerous cleaning products leave behind chemical remnants or do not completely eliminate signs such as blood proteins, drug remnants, or fire starters. Sophisticated methods like LC-MS/MS or luminol testing can uncover what's not visible to the naked eye—even post-cleaning efforts.

7. ***Myth : Chemical outcomes definitively establish guilt or innocence.***

Reality : Chemical evidence aids inquiries but does not establish culpability. A substance discovered at a location does not demonstrate who utilized it. An accelerant found near a fire does not demonstrate intent. Forensic chemists provide impartial information, yet this must be understood within the wider legal and contextual backgroun

An actual case study: The Oklahoma City Bombing – Chemical Evidence in Action

The Heartbreaking Event

On April 19, 1995, a huge truck bomb detonated outside the Alfred P. Murrah Federal Building in Oklahoma City, resulting in the deaths of 168 individuals and wounding hundreds more. The bombing was the most lethal incident of domestic terrorism in U.S. history at that time. Within hours, law enforcement and forensic experts initiated a thorough investigation at the severely damaged location.

The Function of Forensic Chemistry

Investigators in forensic chemistry gathered debris, ash, and residue at the location. Employing methods like gas chromatography-mass spectrometry (GC-MS) and infrared spectroscopy, they determined essential elements of the explosive: a blend of ammonium nitrate and fuel oil (ANFO). Remnants of these substances matched those of homemade explosives and were discovered on fragments from the explosion area, along with items linked to the suspect.

Connecting Evidence to the Suspects

Timothy McVeigh, the main suspect, was apprehended soon after the assault. Chemical analyses subsequently found traces of explosives on his garments and on the remains of a rental vehicle thought to have transported the bomb. These results, along with witness accounts and rental documentation, strengthened the link between McVeigh and the bombing supplies.

Importance in Forensic Chemistry

This instance demonstrated how forensic chemistry can reveal the identity and source of intricate explosive substances, even in tumultuous settings. In spite of the destruction, residual chemical evidence assisted in piecing together the bomb's makeup and connected it to the culprits. It also highlighted the significance of maintaining chain of custody, preserving samples, and employing several confirmatory methods to guarantee dependable, court-admissible outcomes.

In conclusion, Forensic chemistry is a crucial and versatile field within forensic science, often working discreetly behind the scenes to identify poisons, drugs, explosives, and unknown substances.

Although media often exaggerates its potential, the true power of forensic chemistry is found in its accuracy, procedures, and perseverance. It doesn't instantly recognize materials with a mere look, nor does it pass judgments—but it reveals the scientific reality of the chemical proof, which can be a significant influence in both unraveling crimes and protecting the innocent.

CHAPTER 9

EXPERT Q&A

Question : *Is it true that forensic toxicologists can always tell how someone died from chemicals in the body?*

Answer : No, it is not always possible for forensic toxicologists to determine the exact cause of death solely based on the presence of chemicals in the body. While toxicology reports are a vital component of forensic investigations, they primarily provide information about the presence, quantity, and possible effects of substances—such as drugs, alcohol, poisons, or other chemicals—within the body at the time of death.

However, identifying a substance does not automatically explain how or why a person died. Many substances found in the body may be there due to prescribed medication, recreational use, or environmental exposure and may not have contributed directly to the death. For example, therapeutic levels of a drug may be present, but death could have occurred from an unrelated cause, such as trauma, natural disease, or underlying medical conditions.

To accurately determine the cause of death, toxicological findings must be interpreted in conjunction with other critical pieces of evidence, including:Autopsy findings (such as internal injuries, organ damage, or anatomical anomalies)

Medical history (such as chronic illnesses, known substance use, or past treatments)Circumstantial evidence and scene investigation (including how and where the body was found, witness statements, or signs of struggle)

In complex cases, a multidisciplinary approach involving pathologists, toxicologists, and investigators is necessary to form a complete and scientifically valid conclusion.

Ultimately, while forensic toxicologists play a key role by identifying and quantifying substances, determining the actual cause of death often requires a comprehensive, case-by-case analysis that goes beyond the toxicology report alone.

Dinsha K

Assistant professor

Forensic chemistry and pharmacology.

***Question :** Do instruments like GC-MS or FTIR always give a 'perfect' answer?*

Answer: The accuracy and reliability of toxicological analysis are highly dependent on the quality of the sample and the procedures used during testing. If the sample collected for analysis is not of optimal quality—due to contamination, degradation, or improper storage—it can significantly affect the outcome of the results.

Presence of impurities or foreign substances within the sample can interfere with the detection and measurement of the target compounds. These unwanted elements may produce misleading signals during analysis, resulting in false positives, false negatives, or inaccurate concentration levels of the toxic substances being tested.

Similarly, improper sample preparation or poor extraction techniques can compromise the integrity of the analysis. In forensic toxicology, the process of extracting toxic substances from complex biological matrices (like blood, urine, liver tissue, etc.) is a critical step. If the extraction is incomplete, inefficient, or contaminated, it may lead to the loss of important analytes or the co-extraction of interfering compounds, both of which can distort the final interpretation.

Therefore, strict adherence to validated protocols, proper sample handling, and use of high-quality reagents and instruments are essential to ensure the reliability of toxicological findings. Any compromise in these areas not only affects the accuracy of the results but can also hinder the ability of forensic experts to draw valid conclusions, which is especially critical in legal and medico-legal investigations.

Dhanya R

Assistant professor

Department of forensic science

Nehru Arts and Science Colleges

Specialised in Toxicology and pharmacology

Question: *"Is it true that every drug has a unique 'fingerprint' that machines can easily recognize?"*

Answer : Yes, in most cases, drugs exhibit unique "fingerprints" when analyzed using advanced instrumental techniques, which enables their accurate identification and characterization. These analytical"fingerprints"refer to the distinct set of physical or chemical properties that a compound exhibits when subjected to specific methods of analysis. These characteristics are often consistent and reproducible, making them highly valuable in forensic toxicology, pharmaceutical analysis, and quality control.

Analytical instruments such as mass spectrometry (MS), infrared (IR) spectroscopy, nuclear magnetic resonance (NMR), ultraviolet-visible (UV-Vis) spectroscopy, and chromatographic techniques like gas chromatography (GC) and high-performance liquid chromatography (HPLC) are widely used to study these properties.

Each technique provides a different perspective on the compound:

Mass spectrometry (MS) reveals the molecular weight and fragmentation pattern of the drug, offering insights into its molecular structure. Infrared (IR) spectroscopy detects functional groups by measuring molecular vibrations, creating a characteristic absorption spectrum.

Nuclear magnetic resonance (NMR) spectroscopy provides detailed information about the molecular framework, including the arrangement of atoms.

UV-Vis spectroscopy measures electronic transitions, which are useful for identifying conjugated systems in molecules.

Chromatographic methods (GC, HPLC) separate compounds based on their physical or chemical interactions with the mobile and stationary phases, generating retention times unique to each substance under defined conditions.

Even though certain structurally related analogs or isomers may produce similar spectra or chromatographic behavior, a multi-technique approach typically allows for reliable differentiation. For example, two isomers may have overlapping IR spectra but distinct fragmentation patterns in MS or different retention times in chromatography.

By integrating results from multiple analytical techniques, forensic chemists and toxicologists can confidently distinguish between substances—even those that are chemically similar. This multi-layered verification process is essential, especially in forensic cases, where accurate identification of a drug or toxic substance can influence legal outcomes and public health decisions.

Ms. Reshma santhosh

Assistant professor

Dept. Criminology and forensic science

Forensic Toxicology and pharmacology

Question : *"Do gloves completely prevent fingerprints from being left behind?"*

Answer : Though gloves can prevent most of the time the fingerprints to be left behind. But, in some rare cases where either gloves are worn out, torn or damaged gloves that may still allow partial fingerprints to pass through or when made up from textured materials like latex or leather. Sweat or oils can also seep through thin gloves, potentially transferring trace evidence. However, generally speaking, gloves can prevent traditional fingerprints from being left behind by blocking the skin's contact with surfaces. I hope this helps.

Dr Richa Rohatgi

Assistant Professor and Academic Coordinator

School of Forensic Science

NFSU Delhi Campus.

Question: *Is it a myth that all forensic labs have the latest high-tech equipment like we see in crime dramas?*

Answer: Yes, it is a myth that all forensic labs have the latest high-tech equipment like you see in crime dramas such as CSI

Most forensic labs especially those in smaller jurisdictions or underfunded public agencies, operate on tight budgets.

Whereas some federal or state labs might enjoy access to the latest technology, many regional or local labs work with restricted budgets. This frequently results in them having to work with antiquated machines, deciding which cases to analyze first, or sending complicated testing out to specialty labs. In reality, unlike movies and webseries where DNA findings arrive within minutes, actual analysis can take weeks, months, or even days if a lab has a crowded backlog.

Also, not all labs are equipped to conduct all forms of forensic testing. Digital forensic testing, toxicology, or trace evidence testing may require sending the tests to other facilities, adding more time to the process. Forensic scientists are well-educated, but they're not the"do-it-all geniuses"depicted in movies and webseries. The majority are experts in a particular area and have to adhere to rigid procedures and documentation requirements in order to be able to use the evidence in court.

Personnel deficiencies are another problem. Several forensic laboratories have difficulty hiring and keeping skilled employees frequently because of low compensation or heavy workload. This can prolong turnaround time and decrease the volume of cases a lab can process effectively.

In brief, forensic science is an essential component of contemporary law enforcement, but the slick, high-tech, fast moving crime drama world depicted on television does not represent the reality of what many forensic laboratories actually deal with in real life. The actual process is slower, more deliberative, and limited by practical considerations quite far from instant justice so commonly depicted on television

Harsha vardhan Dasari,

lovelydasari890@gmail.com,

Digital forensics and cyber investigation,

Teesside university, Uk

Question: Some say cyber forensics can recover anything, no matter what. Is that an exaggeration?

Answer : Cyber forensics and data recovery are powerful tools, but their success isn't guaranteed. These techniques can often retrieve lost, deleted, or hidden data, but their effectiveness is influenced by many variables. They play a crucial role in investigations, cybersecurity incidents, and legal cases, helping uncover critical digital evidence.

The likelihood of recovering lost data depends on several factors, including the method of data loss, the type of storage device involved (such as HDDs, SSDs, or cloud storage), the actions taken after the data loss (like continued use or attempted recovery), and the sophistication of the tools and expertise used in the recovery process. Each of these elements can significantly impact the outcome.

What can be recovered:

Erased files that haven't been replaced by new data

Storage devices that have been reformatted, though some information might be missing depending on how the format was done. Digital footprints such as activity logs and file details

Bits and pieces of files lingering in unused parts of the storage

Information from faulty or malfunctioning drives, at least in part, with the help of advanced recovery techniques.

Saurav kumar

CYBER Forensic Data Analyst

mishrasaurav463@gmail.com

***Question** : "Do identical twins have the exact same DNA profile, making them impossible to tell apart in forensics?"*

Answer : Identical twins do not have exactly the same DNA profile, though they are extremely similar.

Same:-

Identical twins originate from a single fertilized egg that splits into two, so they have identical nuclear DNA, becouse of this STR Profiling techque cannot distinguish between identical twins.

Difference:-

1. Mutation over time :- Post-zygotic mutations accumulate and can cause minor differences in the DNA of identical twins.

   Advance techniques like Whole Genome Sequencing and Next Generation Sequencing can detect these differences.

2. Epigenetics:- Identical twins can have different epigenetic markers (like DNA methylation patterns), which can be influenced by environment, lifestyle, and disease.

Piyush kumar

Specialised in DNA profiling

piyushchawla824206@gmail.com

Question : *"Is it true that a single piece of evidence, like a hair or fiber, is always enough to convict someone?"*

Answer : No it's not true when it comes to convicting some one or to punish some one hair or fiber is not enough to prove the person as guilty

They are only considered as trace evidence in the court room which may support the investigation but we can't completely depend only on this

Darshan rs

Assistant professor

Mary matha college of arts and science

shivaf334@gmail.com

***Question** : "Can criminals stay hidden if they only use encrypted apps?"*

Answer: No criminal can never stay hidden completely by using encrypted apps.

If the criminals hide the end to end encryption, but the FORENSICS will investigate the metadata.

So,

Encryption hidden words, not actions, criminals can hide their messages, but never their mistakes.

Venkat Gangadari

digital forensic analyst

gangadarivenkatramana10@gmail.com

Question: *"Is it true that all types of forgeries are easily detectable with modern technology?"*

Answer : We cannot say that all forgeries are easily detectable even with modern technology. As detection tools improve so do forgery techniques, especially with the advancements in artificial intelligence they are able to closely mimic genuine documents.

To some extent we are able to detect forgeries but at the same time analytical challenges are also increasing.

Aryasree A

Assistant professor, Forensic Science

aryasreea38@gmail.com

***Question:**"Is it true that livor mortis (postmortem staining) tells exactly how long a person has been dead?"*

Answer : I would like to clarify that livor mortis does not indicate the exact time since death but rather provides an approximate estimation during the early postmortem period. And to be honest i have never seen any forensic medicine expert calculating TSD through LM instead they prefer rectal temperature.

Anurag dubey

Scientific officer

State Forensic science laboratory of karnataka state police

Question: *"Is it a myth that all drug overdoses leave clear and visible symptoms?*

Answer : Yes, it is a myth. Not all drug overdoses result in clear or visible external symptoms. While some may show signs like foaming at the mouth, constricted pupils, or bluish skin, many cases mimic natural death.In many real-world cases—particularly with new psychoactive substances (NPS) or slow-acting poisons—the individual may simply appear drowsy, confused, even just asleep or unconscious. Some drug-related deaths are discovered only through toxicological analysis. The type of drug, dosage, method of intake, and the individual's health condition all play a role in how symptoms appear.

Archana Sunil

Assistant Professor, Department of Forensic Science

a6chanasunil@gmail.com

Question : *Many people believe DNA analysis gives instant results. How long does it actually take, and why?*

Answer : Many people believe that DNA analysis provides instant results, much like what is portrayed in television crime dramas. However, in reality, DNA testing is a complex and time-consuming process that typically takes several days to weeks to complete. After evidence is collected from a crime scene, the DNA must be carefully extracted, purified, and quantified in a laboratory. This is followed by amplification using a process called Polymerase Chain Reaction (PCR), which generates enough DNA for analysis. The amplified DNA is then separated and visualized to create a unique DNA profile. Experts must analyze this profile, often comparing it with reference samples or searching it against national databases. Each of these steps requires careful attention to detail, strict protocols, and quality control measures to ensure the results are accurate and legally admissible. Additionally, backlogs in forensic labs, especially in high-demand regions, can significantly extend the time it takes to process a sample. While simple cases with high-quality samples might be completed in a few days, complex or degraded samples can take several weeks or even longer. Thus, the idea of instant DNA results is a myth; the actual process is thorough, deliberate, and designed to ensure the integrity of forensic evidence.

Nidhin SS

Assistant professor

Department of forensic science

Specialised in forensic serology and DNA profiling

***Question:** Does the type of paper or ink used provide clues about when and where a document was made?*

Answer :

Yes,the type of paper and ink used in a document can provide significant clues about its origin and age.Forensic document examination employs various analytical techniques to assess thesematerials,aiding in the determination of when and where a document was created.

Paper Analysis

Paper is composed of fibers(commonly cellulose from wood pulp or cotton),fillers,and chemical additives.The nature and treatment of these components can provide time-specific and location-specific information.

1.Paper Composition and Characteristics

The composition of paper—including the type of fibers,fillers,and additives,can indicate its manufacturing period and origin.For instance,the presence of certain optical brighteningagents (OBAs)in paper can suggest a production date,as these agents were introduced in themid-20th century.

·Optical Brightening Agents(OBAs):These chemicals were introduced in the mid-20th century to make paper appear whiter under UV light.Their presence can rule out earlier dates of origin(Legal Desire,2022).

· Watermarks:These embedded designs,often visible when held to light,can be traced tospecific manufacturers and time periods.

·Paper Formation:Handmade paper,prevalent before the 19th century,differs substantially from the uniform texture of machine-made paper.

2.Paper Aging and Environmental Factors

Environmental factors such as exposure to light,humidity,and temperature can cause paper to age,leading to changes in color and texture.By analysing these changes,forensic experts can estimate the time elapsed since the document was created.

Ink Analysis:

Ink Chemical Composition and Dating Inks are composed of various dyes,pigments,solvents,and additives.By analysing the chemical composition of ink,forensic scientists can determine its formulation and compare it with known standards to estimate the period when it was manufactured.Techniques like High Performance Liquid Chromatography(HPLC)and Gas Chromatography-Mass Spectrometry (GC-MS)are commonly used for this purpose.

·Raman Spectroscopy and Ink Degradation Raman spectroscopy is a non-destructive technique that can assess the degradation of ink over time.By examining changes in the Raman spectra of ink,researchers can estimate the age of the writing.For example,studies have shown that the degradation of certain ink components follows predictable patterns,allowing for age estimation.

·Thin-Layer Chromatography (TLC)for Ink Comparison

TLC is a widely used method for comparing ink samples.It separates the components of ink based on their chemical properties,providing a"fingerprint"that can be compared between questioned and known samples.This technique is particularly useful for identifying the type of ink used and detecting alterations or additions to a document.

·Mass Spectrometry and Spectroscopy:Gas Chromatography-Mass Spectrometry (GC-MS)and Raman spectroscopy are used to analyse ink aging through degradation patterns.

The Vinland Map:Uncovering a Historical Forgery One of the most famous instances of forensic ink analysis occurred in the case of the Vinland Map,a document allegedly dating back to the 15th century that purported to show Norse

exploration of North America before Columbus.For decades,the map was a subject of debate among historians and scientists.

However,forensic testing ultimately revealed that the ink used on the map contained anatase, a crystalline form of titanium dioxide that was not commercially available before the 20th century.Raman spectroscopy and other techniques confirmed this anomaly,conclusively proving the map to be a modern forgery.This case is a prime example of how chemical ink analysis can expose attempts to falsify historical narratives(McCrone,1974;Garman et al.,2002).

Manju,

Scientific Officer at SIFS India

Manjusihag11@gmail.com

Question: *"Some say that hair analysis can give a perfect, reliable drug history over months. How true is this?"*

answer : Hair analysis has a detection window of up to 90 days for head hair and maybe up to a year for body hair, making it a useful tool for identifying chronic drug use. It is not a perfect or conclusive indicator of a person's drug past, despite its value. This approach is not appropriate for detecting recent use since drug metabolites build up in hair gradually and usually become detectable only 7–10 days after intake.

Hair testing's sensitivity dramatically drops for substances that are used seldom, like cannabis, where detection rates can be as low as 50% in infrequent users. In contrast, drugs like cocaine and opioids can be reliably detected. False positives or negative results can also be caused by outside variables such as environmental contamination, hair color, and cosmetic procedures like bleaching and dying. Legal and medical experts also advise against relying too much on hair test findings without taking into account individual characteristics like hair texture, ethnicity, or grooming habits.

The method's strengths in timeline reconstruction have been emphasized by research, especially when employing sophisticated approaches like micro-segmental analysis. By calculating the exact timing of zolpidem administration in a drug-facilitated crime instance, one case study prominently illustrated this. For a thorough understanding of both recent and past drug exposure, experts concur that hair testing works best when combined with other biological matrices, such as blood or urine. To sum up, hair analysis is an effective clinical and forensic technique for monitoring long-term drug trends, but it needs to be used carefully and understood contextually. It is not sufficient evidence of drug use on its own.

Ms. Vineeshma M

Assistant Professor

Department of Criminology and Forensic Science

NASC

References :

Bevel, T.,&Gardner, R. M. (2008). Bloodstain pattern analysis with an introduction to crime scene reconstruction (3rd ed.). CRC Press.

Butler, J. M. (2015). Advanced topics in forensic DNA typing: Interpretation. Academic Press.

Champod, C., Lennard, C., Margot, P.,&Stoilovic, M. (2004). Fingerprints and other ridge skin impressions. CRC Press.

Dean, J. R. (2003). Practical instrumental analysis. Wiley.

DiMaio, V. J.,&DiMaio, D. (2001). Forensic pathology (2nd ed.). CRC Press.

Houck, M. M. (2009). Trace evidence analysis: More cases in forensic microscopy and mute witnesses. Academic Press.

Houck, M. M.,&Siegel, J. A. (2015). Fundamentals of forensic science (3rd ed.). Academic Press.

Jobling, M. A.,&Gill, P. (2004). Encoded evidence: DNA in forensic analysis. Nature Reviews Genetics, 5(10), 739–751. https://doi.org/10.1038/nrg1455

Karch, S. B. (2016). Drug abuse handbook (3rd ed.). CRC Press.

Levine, B. (2010). Principles of forensic toxicology (4th ed.). AACC Press.

Robertson, J.,&Roux, C. (2010). Trace evidence: Here today, gone tomorrow? Science&Justice, 50(1), 18–22. https://doi.org/10.1016/j.scijus.2009.11.001

Rouessac, F.,&Rouessac, A. (2013). Chemical analysis: Modern instrumentation methods and techniques (2nd ed.). Wiley.

Saferstein, R. (2018). Forensic science: From the crime scene to the crime lab (4th ed.). Pearson.

Saks, M. J.,&Koehler, J. J. (2005). The coming paradigm shift in forensic identification science. Science, 309(5736), 892–895. https://doi.org/10.1126/science.1111565

Spitz, W. U. (2006). Spitz and Fisher's medicolegal investigation of death: Guidelines for the application of pathology to crime investigation (4th ed.). Charles C Thomas Publisher.

Tebbett, I. R. (1999). Introduction to forensic chemistry. CRC Press.

Meyer, R. (2013). The role of forensic chemistry in criminal investigations. Wiley-VCH.

Bell, S. (2012). Forensic chemistry (2nd ed.). Pearson.

Croom, E. M. (1995). Essence of herbal medicine: The principles and chemistry of medicinal plants. Pharmacy Books.

De Forest, P. R., Gaensslen, R. E.,&Lee, H. C. (1983). Forensic science: An introduction to criminalistics. McGraw-Hill.

Eisenberg, A. (2019). Chemistry matters: Forensic science. Lerner Publications.

Jackson, A. R. W.,&Jackson, J. M. (2011). Forensic science (3rd ed.). Pearson Education.

Miller, M. L.,&Basset, C. G. (2014). Introduction to criminalistics: The foundation of forensic science. Elsevier.

Ogle, R. R.,&Watson, K. A. (2012). Crime scene investigation and reconstruction (3rd ed.). Pearson.

Palenik, S. J. (2000). Microscopic particle examination — an introduction to forensic trace evidence. Journal of Forensic Sciences, 45(5), 990–1001. https://doi.org/10.1520/JFS14812J

Wallace, H. (2009). Forensic science and the criminal justice system: Improvements and challenges. Australian Institute of Criminology. https://www.aic.gov.au

Kellogg, S. (2013). Analytical chemistry for forensic science. Wiley.

Moore, D. S. (2004). Instrumentation in forensic chemistry: Trends and applications. Analytical Chemistry, 76(20), 6267–6285.

Zarbl, H. (2010). Modern techniques in forensic chemistry. Annual Review of Analytical Chemistry, 3, 359–382. https://doi.org/10.1146/annurev.anchem.111808.073703